SPACE
EXPLORATION

DAVID GLOVER

How to use this book

Cross references
Above the heading on the page, you will find a list of other pages in the book which are connected to the topic. Look at these pages to find out more about the topic.

See for yourself
See for yourself bubbles give you the chance to test out some of the ideas in this book. They explain what you will need and what you have to do to see if an idea really works.

Quiz corner
In the quiz corner, you will find a list of questions. The answers to the quiz questions are somewhere on the two pages. Can you answer all the questions about each topic?

Glossary
Words that may be difficult to understand are marked in **bold**. These words are explained in the glossary near the back of the book. If you do not understand a bold word, look in the glossary to see what it means.

Index
The index is at the back of the book. It is a list of important words and subjects mentioned in the book, with page numbers next to the words. The list is in the same order as the alphabet. If you want to find out about a subject, look up the word in the index, then turn to the page number given.

Contents

What is space?

When you look up at the stars on a clear night, you are looking out into space. Stars, planets, **moons**, **comets** and **asteroids** are all part of space. The whole of space and everything in it, including Earth, is called the universe.

Our planet
We live on a planet called Earth, which is a ball of rock and metal moving through space. Earth seems big to us, but compared with the universe it is tiny.

SEE FOR YOURSELF
On a clear night, use a pair of binoculars to look more closely at the night sky. Put on some warm clothes and tell an adult you are going outside. Then make yourself comfortable and watch the spectacular show.

Learning about space
Scientists called astronomers study the stars and planets. They use powerful **telescopes** to look out at space. To see even further into space, rockets launch spacecraft to visit other planets. These spacecraft send close-up pictures of the planets and their moons back to Earth.

◀ People who travel into space are called astronauts. They wear special suits to protect their bodies and to help them breathe.

Bright stars
There are millions of stars in space. Stars look like tiny pinpoints of light, but really they are huge balls of burning gas. Our Sun is a star. It looks brighter than all the other stars because it is closer to Earth.

WARNING:
Never look straight at the Sun with or without binoculars. It is so bright that it will damage your eyes.

Quiz Corner

- Name three things you find in space.

- What is Earth made of?

- Why does the Sun seem brighter than other stars?

- What do astronomers do?

▷ Thousands of years ago, people saw the same display of stars that you see today.

The solar system is the name we give to the Sun and all the things that go round, or **orbit**, it. These include nine planets and more than 60 **moons**. Many smaller objects that orbit the Sun, such as **comets** and **asteroids**, are also part of the solar system.

The planets
The nine planets of the solar system are different sizes and are at different distances from the Sun. Mercury is the closest, then Venus, Earth, Mars, Jupiter, Saturn, Uranus, Neptune and Pluto. They all orbit at different speeds. It takes one year for Earth to go round the Sun once.

▷ This illustration shows the sizes of the planets compared with each other. The spaces between each of the planets are much greater than shown here.

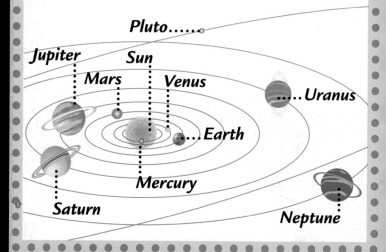

Gravity and orbits
On Earth, a force called **gravity** pulls all objects towards the planet's surface. Larger objects in space, such as the Sun, have a stronger pull of gravity. The Sun's gravity keeps the planets in their orbits and stops them floating off further into space.

Pluto......

Jupiter   Sun

Mars   Venus

........Uranus

........Earth

Mercury

Saturn   Neptune

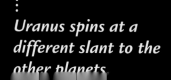

Pluto is the smallest planet, even smaller than our Moon.

Neptune is a blue planet, covered in places by wispy white clouds.

Uranus spins at a different slant to the other planets.

Saturn has many beautiful rings around its middle.

HATTERB

All the planets, apart from Earth, are named after Greek or Roman gods. Venus was the Roman goddess of love, Neptune was the Roman god of the sea and Uranus was the Greek god of the universe.

Mercury is only slightly bigger than our Moon.

Venus is wrapped in thick, poisonous clouds.

Earth's surface is mostly covered with water.

The Sun is a the centre of the solar system.

Mars looks red when seen from Earth.

Asteroids and comets
Asteroids are lumps of rock in space. Millions of asteroids orbit the Sun between Mars and Jupiter. Comets are balls of snow and dus that follow an oval-shaped orbit, rather than a circular orbit, round the Sun. Wher a comet is close to the Sun, the snow turns to gas and makes a long tail.

Quiz Corner

- Which is the smallest planet?
- What is at the centre of the solar system?
- How long does Earth take to orbit the Sun?
- What is a comet's tail made of?

Jupiter is the largest planet and, after Venus, is the easiest planet to spot in the night sky.

look at: Stars and galaxies, page 14, Rockets, page 20

Sun and Moon

The Sun is millions of kilometres away from Earth. Even from this distance, its heat and light warm our planet and make plants grow. The Moon is a cold ball of rock that moves round Earth. It is about four times smaller than Earth and 400 times smaller than the Sun. There is no air, no water and no life on the Moon.

Days and nights
While Earth **orbits** the Sun, it spins – once every 24 hours. We call this length of time one day. When the side of Earth where you live faces the Sun, it is daytime. When it is turned away from the Sun, it is night-time.

.... *daytime*

.... *night-time*

▲ As Earth spins from day into night, the Sun starts to disappear from view.

► In the same way that Earth orbits the Sun, the Moon orbits Earth.

The changing Moon
The Moon looks bright in the night sky, but it does not give out its own light. It shines because, like a mirror, it **reflects** light from the Sun. Each night, the Moon appears to be a slightly different shape. This is because our view of the sunlit side of the Moon changes as it orbits Earth.

▼ Every month, the Moon takes about two weeks to go from new to full. It takes another two weeks to become new again.

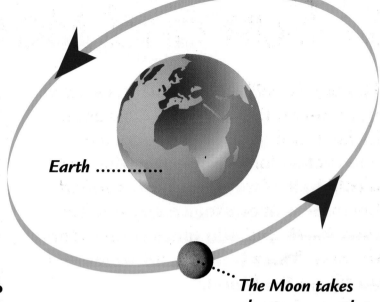

Earth ············

The Moon takes about one month to orbit Earth once.

New Moon

Crescent Moon

First quarter

Full Moon

SEE FOR YOURSELF

*The Moon is covered with huge hollows called **craters**. These are made when objects crash into the Moon's surface. Fill a bowl with flour and drop in some pebbles. Take the pebbles away and discover your own Moon surface.*

Quiz Corner

● How long does it take Earth to make one full spin?

● How long does it take the Moon to orbit Earth?

● Which is larger – the Sun or the Moon?

look at: The solar system, page 6, Reaching the planets, page 26

Rocky planets

The four planets closest to the Sun – Mercury, Venus, Earth and Mars – are called rocky planets. They are balls of rock with metal cores. Pluto, the furthest planet from the Sun, is also a rocky planet. It is thought to be made entirely of rock.

▼ Mercury has many mountains and **craters**. It looks similar to the Moon, but it is much hotter.

CHATTERBOX

So far, scientists have no proof that there is life on any planet except Earth. In 1976, the Viking spacecraft landed on Mars and found no signs of life. But scientists still believe that there may have been life on Mars millions of years ago, when there was flowing water on the planet.

▶ The hot surface of Venus is covered with rocky mountains and wide craters. Thick clouds make the sky orange.

Inside Earth

Earth's surface is called the crust. Below the crust, there is a layer of rock called the mantle. Below this, there is a layer of hot liquid metal called the outer core. Earth's centre, or inner core, is solid metal.

.... *crust*

.... *mantle*

.... *outer core*

.... *inner core*

Mercury and Venus

As Mercury turns to face the Sun, the **temperature** becomes hot enough to melt lead. At night, as Mercury turns away from the Sun, the land becomes freezing. Venus is further away from the Sun than Mercury, but its surface is hotter. The heat is trapped by a layer of gas which surrounds Venus.

Earth and Mars

Earth is at just the right distance from the Sun for life to exist. It is neither too hot, nor too cold. As far as we know, it is the only planet that has flowing water. Mars is smaller than Earth and much colder. There is water on Mars, but it is frozen at the top and bottom of the planet.

Pluto

Pluto was discovered in 1930. It has one **moon**, which is almost as big as Pluto itself. Pluto is still a mystery to astronomers – so far, it has not been explored by any spacecraft.

Quiz Corner

- What are the names of the rocky planets?

- Has life been discovered anywhere other than on Earth?

- What is at the centre of Earth?

- How many moons does Pluto have?

look at: The solar system, page 6, Reaching the planets, page 26

Gas planets

Jupiter, Saturn, Uranus and Neptune are often called the gas giants. They are large planets made of gas and liquids. All of the gas planets have rings made up of pieces of rock. Astronauts have not visited these planets because they are too far away and do not have a hard surface where they can land.

▶ Saturn has the most spectacular rings of all the gas planets.

As Saturn spins,.. winds blow the gases around the planet into stripes.

▼ Jupiter is a bright orange planet with one narrow ring.

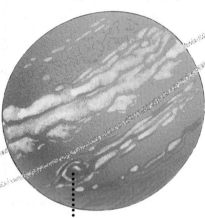

Great Red Spot

Jupiter and Saturn

Jupiter is the largest planet in the solar system. It is 11 times bigger than Earth. Jupiter spins faster than the other planets and fierce storms rage on its surface. One of these, called the Great Red Spot, has lasted for over 300 years. Saturn is the second largest planet and has at least 22 **moons**. Three of its bright rings can be seen from Earth with a **telescope**.

▼ Uranus is surrounded by a thick blue layer of gas.

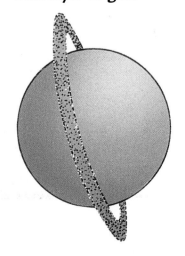

▼ Neptune is slightly smaller than Uranus and is the furthest gas giant from the Sun.

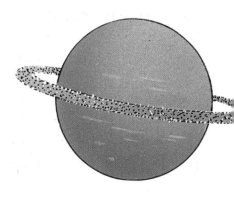

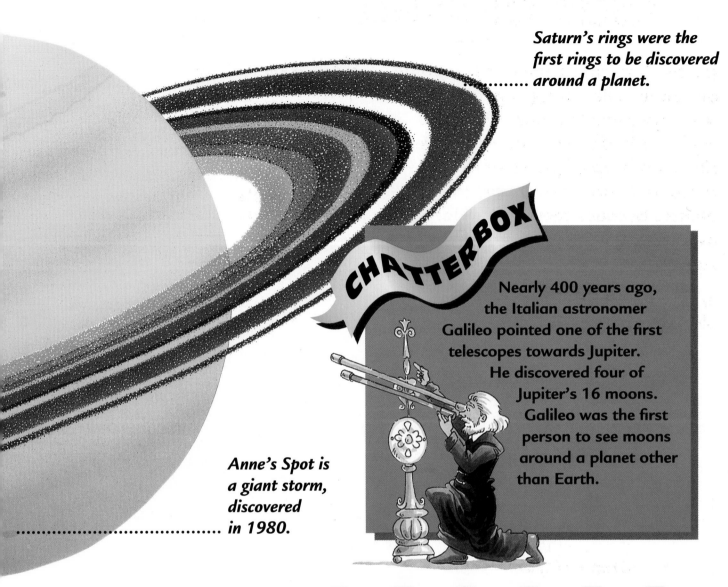

Saturn's rings were the first rings to be discovered .... around a planet.

CHATTERBOX

Nearly 400 years ago, the Italian astronomer Galileo pointed one of the first telescopes towards Jupiter. He discovered four of Jupiter's 16 moons. Galileo was the first person to see moons around a planet other than Earth.

Anne's Spot is a giant storm, discovered .... in 1980.

Uranus and Neptune
Uranus has at least 15 moons. It is the only gas planet on which astronomers have not found clouds or storms. On Neptune, winds blow at over three times the speed of the strongest winds on Earth. Triton, Neptune's largest moon, is the coldest place in the solar system.

Quiz Corner

- Which is the largest planet in the solar system?
- How many moons does Saturn have?
- Where is the coldest place in the solar system?

look at: Constellations, page 16

Stars and galaxies

Stars are balls of gas that burn for millions of years. Each one belongs to a huge spinning group of stars called a **galaxy**. The Sun and all the stars we see in the sky are part of a galaxy called the Milky Way. It is one of billions of galaxies in space.

Big distances
Most stars in the Milky Way are so far away that even if you travelled in an aeroplane for one million years you would not reach them. Their light takes hundreds of years to reach us. The light from one distant star may take so long to reach us that by the time we see it, the star itself has died.

▼ Stars are born from a huge cloud of gas and dust called a **nebula**.

A star is born
Over millions of years, gas and dust in a nebula are pulled into a ball by **gravity**. The ball heats up and glows as a bright star. As the gas runs out, the star begins to die.

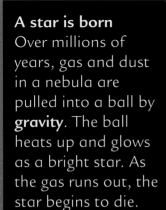

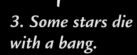

1. A star comes to life.

2. After millions of years, the star grows and begins to turn red.

3. Some stars die with a bang.

▼ **Our galaxy, the Milky Way, is shaped like a spiral.**

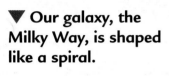

The centre of the Milky Way is hidden by a fog of stardust.

Our solar system is near the edge of the Milky Way.

Moving through space
Some galaxies have spiral arms, others are oval-shaped and others are uneven. Like all objects in space, galaxies spin. Astronomers have discovered that they are moving away from each other, travelling further into space.

Quiz Corner

● What is the name of our galaxy?

● How long do stars live for?

● What shape is our galaxy?

● How many galaxies are there in space?

look at: Stars and galaxies, page 14

Constellations

When you look at the night sky, the bright stars seem to make patterns. In ancient times, people named these patterns after animals, heroes and gods. Today, we call these patterns constellations and use them to make maps of the night sky.

Half and half
Earth is divided into two halves called hemispheres. People who live in the northern hemisphere see a different set of stars to people who live in the southern hemisphere.

...... *northern hemisphere*

...... *southern hemisphere*

Spinning round
Throughout the year, as Earth **orbits** the Sun, the constellations seem to move through the sky. In the northern hemisphere, one star appears to stay in the same place. This star is called the Pole Star because it is always directly above the North Pole. Sailors and other travellers use it to find their way at night.

▼ Here are some constellations you can see from parts of the northern hemisphere, such as Europe, North America and China.

Great Bear

Little Bear

Pole Star

Queen Cassiopeia

King Cepheus

Dragon

Buy a simple star map called a planisphere to help you spot constellations in the night sky. Use it to find out which constellations appear at different times of the year.

Quiz Corner

- What are patterns of stars called?

- What is a planisphere?

- Which constellation includes the Pole Star?

- Name some constellations in the southern hemisphere.

▼ Here are some constellations you can see from parts of the southern hemisphere, such as Australia and parts of South America.

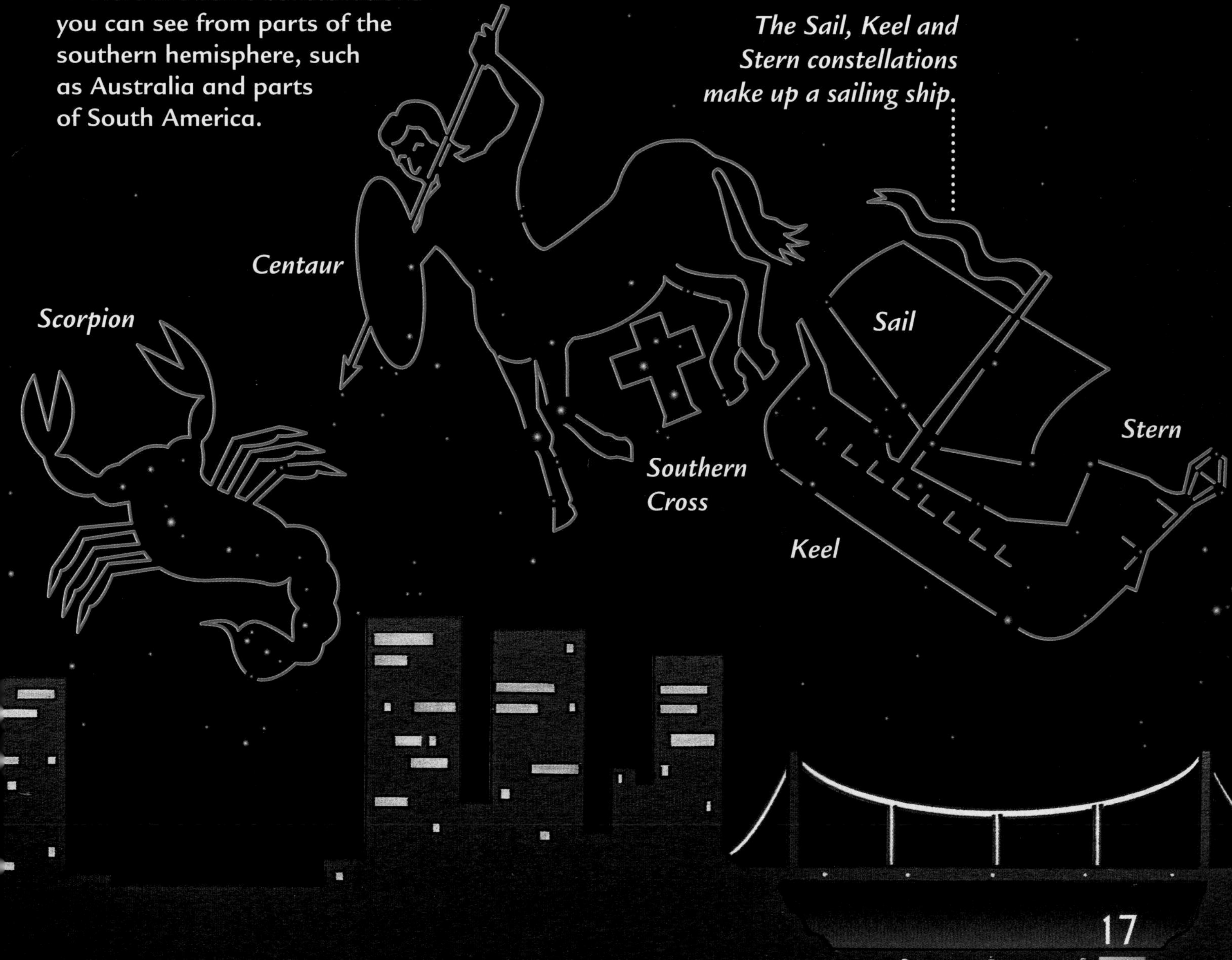

The Sail, Keel and Stern constellations make up a sailing ship.

Centaur

Scorpion

Sail

Stern

Southern Cross

Keel

look at: Rockets, page 20, Space stations, page 24

Being an astronaut

Astronauts travel into space to repair equipment, to carry out experiments or simply to explore. In 1961, the Russian Yuri Gagarin became the first astronaut in space when he **orbited** Earth in the spacecraft Vostok 1. Since then, many astronauts have spent weeks or even months living in space.

CHATTERBOX

In space, people can move around without much effort. Standing, sitting and even running are so easy that muscles begin to lose their strength. To stay fit, astronauts work out regularly on special machines.

Feeling weightless

Far away from Earth, where spacecraft travel, astronauts do not feel **gravity**. Things float in mid-air unless they are fixed to something else. All equipment inside the spacecraft has to be stored in cupboards or attached to walls.

Space suits

A space suit protects an astronaut from the chill of space and the heat of the Sun's rays. There is no air to breathe in space, so an astronaut's space suit is filled with **oxygen** for breathing.

▶ To move freely outside the craft, an astronaut can be strapped into a moving chair called a Manned Manoeuvring Unit, or MMU.

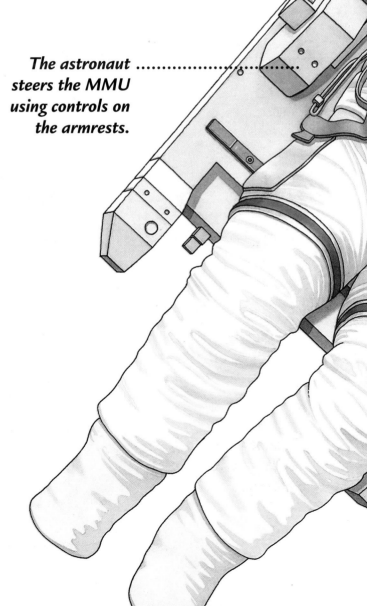

The astronaut .... steers the MMU using controls on the armrests.

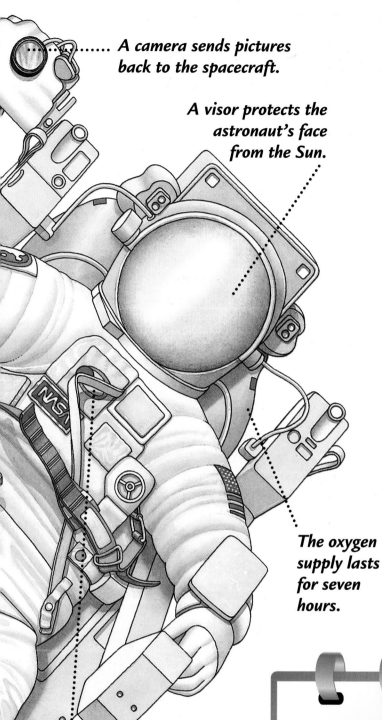

A camera sends pictures back to the spacecraft.

A visor protects the astronaut's face from the Sun.

The oxygen supply lasts for seven hours.

A chest pack carries the computer controls.

▲ Some of an astronaut's training takes place under water where, as in space, everything feels lighter.

Astronaut school

It takes years of training to prepare for a journey into space. Astronauts learn how to use equipment which will keep them alive in space. They need to be able to cope with any emergency. They also practise experiments which they will carry out on board their spacecraft.

Quiz Corner
● Who was the first person in space?

● What does an astronaut need to learn before going into space?

● Where do astronauts do some of their training?

look at: Space shuttles, page 22

Rockets

Rocket power is used to launch all kinds of spacecraft, such as **satellites** and **space shuttles**. A rocket needs tremendous power to lift its load away from Earth and into space. **Fuel** burns inside the rocket and hot gases rush out of the bottom. This jet of fiery heat pushes the rocket upwards.

▶ Ariane 5 is Europe's biggest rocket. It can carry up to four satellites into space.

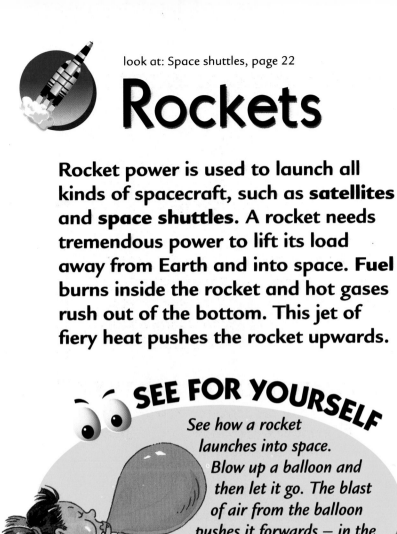

SEE FOR YOURSELF

See how a rocket launches into space. Blow up a balloon and then let it go. The blast of air from the balloon pushes it forwards — in the same way that hot gases push a rocket up into space.

Satellites in space

A satellite is a spacecraft, without people on board, that **orbits** Earth. Rockets launch all kinds of satellites. A space **telescope** is a satellite that looks out into space. It sends information about stars and **galaxies** to Earth. A weather satellite takes pictures of Earth to help people predict the weather.

Launching a satellite

Ariane 5 is made up of two **booster rockets** and two main sections called stages. After take-off, the booster rockets and first stage fall away.

second stage

first stage

booster
.... _rocket_

1. When the booster rockets have run out of fuel, they fall away.

2. The protective covering comes away.

3. The first stage separates and the second stage carries the satellite into space.

▲ Only 12 people have ever walked on the Moon. The first, Neil Armstrong, planted an American flag.

First to the Moon

In 1969, a huge American rocket launched a spacecraft called Apollo 11 towards the Moon. After the rocket stages fell away, Apollo 11 carried the astronauts near to the Moon. Then the spacecraft sent a lander carrying two astronauts, Neil Armstrong and Buzz Aldrin, down to the Moon's surface. They became the first people to land on the Moon.

Quiz Corner

● What do rockets carry into space?

● What is the name of Europe's biggest rocket?

● Who were the first two people to walk on the Moon?

look at: Rockets, page 20, Space stations, page 24

Space shuttles

A **space shuttle** is a spacecraft that can be used more than once. Shuttles have taken many astronauts to space and back. They also deliver **cargo** to **space stations**, returning with equipment in need of repair or with the results of experiments.

▶ A shuttle is launched by two **booster rockets** and a huge **fuel** tank which fall away after take-off.

The cargo bay
Satellites and other pieces of equipment are stored in a large area in the top of the shuttle called the cargo bay. Satellites can be launched or repaired using a robot arm which reaches out of the cargo bay.

Life on board
A trip on the shuttle lasts about nine days. Astronauts breathe the air inside the shuttle and do not need space suits. They sleep in bunks or in bags strapped to the walls. Without the straps, the astronauts would float around.

◀ Before the shuttle lands on Earth, the pilot turns off its engines. It lands in a similar way to an aeroplane, but needs a longer runway.

▶ In 1990, a space shuttle launched the Hubble Space Telescope. It sends pictures of stars and **galaxies** to Earth.

Quiz Corner

- What is kept in the shuttle's cargo bay?

- What is the shuttle's robot arm used for?

- Do astronauts need to wear space suits inside the shuttle?

- Where do astronauts sleep?

This astronaut is using the shuttle's robot arm to help repair part of the Hubble Space Telescope.

look at: Being an astronaut, 18, Space shuttles, page 22

Space stations

A **space station** is a large spacecraft where astronauts live and carry out experiments. In the future, space stations may be used as factories where special materials and medicines will be made. Space stations may also become the starting points for trips to the planets.

Mir space station

In 1986, the Russians launched a space station called Mir. It is made up of different parts, called modules, which were launched by rockets and fitted together in space. There are always astronauts on Mir – some spend over a year on board before returning to Earth.

▼ Here, the spacecraft Soyuz is docking with the main module of Mir.

Spacecraft, such as Soyuz, bring astronauts to Mir.

New modules join with Mir at the docking port.

Astronauts climb through a hatch to enter Mir from the docking port.

CHATTERBOX

Astronauts on Mir have to be careful not to let their food float away while they are eating. It might get into important equipment.

Extra rooms

Each of Mir's modules is used for different activities. The main module is the living area, while a smaller module is used as a space **observatory**. The MMU, used by astronauts to make repairs outside the station, is stored in a separate module.

▶ Mir's final module was added in 1996. Today, space shuttles carry astronauts and equipment to Mir.

Panels on each side of the station use the Sun's rays to make electricity.

Inside Mir, astronauts do not have to wear space suits.

Astronauts eat, sleep and work in Mir's main module.

Accidents in space

In 1997, a delivery craft crashed into the side of Mir. Luckily, nobody was hurt but many experiments were lost. In the future, scientists hope to build a larger and safer space station, called International Space Station, which may be connected to Mir.

Quiz corner

● How long have some astronauts stayed on Mir?

● Where do Mir's new modules join on to the main module?

● How does Mir make electricity?

● What happened to Mir in 1997?

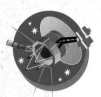

look at: Rocky planets, page 10, Gas planets, page 12

Reaching the planets

Astronauts have travelled only as far as the Moon, but scientists can explore the planets using machines called space probes. These send information and pictures back to scientists on Earth. Space probes have landed on, or flown by, all of the planets in the solar system apart from Pluto.

▼ Probes have landed on Mars and sent back detailed pictures of its rocky, red surface.

Voyager 2
The Voyager 2 probe was launched in 1977. It has flown around Jupiter, Saturn, Uranus and Neptune, beaming pictures of the planets and their **moons** back to Earth. It is now heading out of the solar system and into outer space.

Saturn

Jupiter

Earth

Uranus

Neptune

Searching for life
Voyager 2 carries a special recording, called 'Sounds of Earth', which is a greeting to any living creatures who might find the probe. The recording has words in more than 60 languages and music from countries all over the world.

26

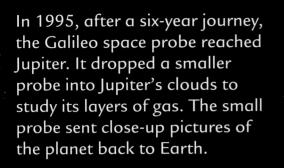

In 1995, after a six-year journey, the Galileo space probe reached Jupiter. It dropped a smaller probe into Jupiter's clouds to study its layers of gas. The small probe sent close-up pictures of the planet back to Earth.

Quiz Corner

- Which planets has Voyager 2 visited?
- What does the surface of Mars look like?
- How long did it take Galileo to reach Jupiter?

◀ After Galileo released the small probe, it **orbited** Jupiter, visiting four of its moons.

look at: Rockets, page 20

Space science

Space exploration is only possible because of the work of scientists. They are continuing to make new rockets and space probes to help us find out more about the universe. While scientists are designing space equipment, they discover many new materials which can be useful on Earth as well as in space.

▶ These runners' capes are made of a material first designed for astronauts' clothing.

Learning from space

We now know much more about how stars and planets are made and about how the universe began. Space science has also changed our everyday lives. Smoke detectors, fire-proof clothing, and lightweight materials for safety helmets and tennis shoes, are all the result of research into space travel.

▼ One day, astronauts might visit Mars. This is how some scientists imagine Mars might look in the future.

Communication

Some **satellites** are launched into space to help people on Earth communicate with each other. They can bounce telephone or television signals almost instantly from one side of Earth to the other.

1 A caller speaks into a telephone in the USA.

2 The signal bounces off the satellite.

3 The signal reaches the person in Africa.

People and animals would need to wear space suits.

Plants in giant greenhouses would provide some of the food.

Quiz Corner

● What are communication satellites used for?

● How many inventions can you name that were a result of space science?

● Which planet might people visit in the future?

People would travel to other parts of Mars on a special lander.

Cars would need thick tyres to cope with the rough Martian landscape.

People would use dishes to send messages to Earth by satellite.

Amazing facts

● Scientists believe that the universe was made 15 billion years ago by a huge explosion called the Big Bang.

☆ *Radio waves carrying our radio and television programmes never disappear. They journey into space, travelling millions of kilometres each year. One day, life on distant planets – if there is any – could tune into our shows!*

● The highest mountain in the solar system is Olympus Mons on Mars. It is three times higher than Mount Everest.

☆ *People are taller in space. On Earth, gravity holds the bones of our bodies closer together. In space, people don't feel gravity, so there are gaps between their bones.*

● Story Musgrave, an American, is one of the world's most experienced astronauts. In 1996, at 61 years old, he became the oldest astronaut to travel in space.

☆ *Stars are different colours depending on how hot they are. The hottest stars are blue and the next hottest are blue-white or white. Stars that have a medium heat are yellow, while the coolest ones are red.*

● The most distant stars you can see without a **telescope** are in the Andromeda **galaxy**. Light from this galaxy takes more than two million years to reach Earth.

☆ *The first animal in space was a dog called Laika. She flew on the Russian **satellite** Sputnik 2 in 1957.*

● People used to think that the dark areas on the Moon were seas. We now know that they are huge patches of dark rock.

☆ *Scientists have sent a radio message to a group of stars called M13. The message will take 25,000 years to arrive, so we cannot expect a reply for at least 50,000 years.*

Glossary

asteroid A piece of rock that **orbits** the Sun.

booster rocket This gives extra power for lift-off. It falls away seconds after the main rocket has been launched.

cargo The equipment, food and other goods that spacecraft carry.

comet A ball of snow and dust which moves around the Sun.

crater A hollow in a planet or a **moon**, made by objects crashing into its surface.

fuel A material that burns in an engine and makes it work.

galaxy A group of millions of stars.

gravity The force that makes things fall or have weight. All planets and stars have gravity.

moon An object in space that travels round a planet. A moon is smaller than its planet.

nebula A cloud of gas and dust in space.

observatory A place where astronomers use **telescopes** and other machines to study space.

orbit The curved path of an object in space as it travels round a larger object. Earth orbits the Sun, while the Moon orbits Earth.

oxygen A gas in the air. Animals and plants need oxygen to live.

reflect To bounce light back. We see the Moon because it reflects light from the Sun.

satellite A machine that **orbits** Earth.

space shuttle A spacecraft which can be used more than once.

space station A spacecraft that **orbits** Earth with people on board. Astronauts work here for several months.

telescope A tube with glass lenses or curved mirrors which makes things look bigger and clearer.

temperature How hot or cold something is.

Index

Published by Two-Can Publishing, 43-45 Dorset Street, London W1U 7NA

© 2002 Two-Can Publishing

For information on Two-Can books and multimedia, call (0)20 7224 2440, fax (020 7224 7005, or visit our website at http://www.two-canpublishing.com

Managing Editor: Robert Sved
Art Director: Carole Orbell
Senior Designer: Gareth Dobson
Editor: Janet De Saulles
Picture research: Laura Cartwright
Consultant: Carole Stott
Artwork: Stuart Trotter, Teri Gower, Mel Pickering, Jason Lewis
Production: Adam Wilde
Additional Research: Inga Phipps

Hardback ISBN 1-84301-056-9
Paperback ISBN 1-84301-008-9

Dewey Decimal Classification 523.1

Hardback 2 4 6 8 10 9 7 5 3 1
Paperback 2 4 6 8 10 9 7 5 3 1

A catalogue record for this book is available from the British Library.

Printed and bound in Spain by Graficromo S.A.

Photographic credits: front cover: Pictor; p4: Planet Earth Pictures; p8: Planet Earth Pictures; p10: NASA/Science Photo Library; p14: Royal Observatory, Edinburgh/AAO/Science Photo Library; p19: NASA/Science Photo Library; p22(t): Pictor International; p22(b): NASA/Science Photo Library; p23: Planet Earth Pictures; p25, p26: NASA; p29: PA News.